THE D/UE LAW:
The Massive Loss of Market Income, Resulting From The Lack of Employment

By

Jim Green

DEDICATED TO:
The unvarnished truth:

The purpose of this book is to identify a yet to be discussed LAW…. THE LAW OF DIMINISHED INCOME TO THE MARKET FROM UNEMPLOYMENT [the 8 million the DOL reports are looking for work, but *NO* work exists] , that adversely impacts our economy every day—but to keep our Job Creation on the plantation—is never discussed…..and as well, when we speak of unemployment the mind automatically defaults to the plight of the jobless [and as it rightfully should]—but equally pernicious is the massive loss of income to the Market as a result of unemployment—people do not buy what we manufacture, when they are jobless—i.e., unemployment is a <u>*NO ONE WINS*</u>—Common Sense: And obvious, except for those in our autocracy who are rigid—who still have one foot on the plantation—and see American employees as A POOL OF SLAVES: To Be Used And Discarded "at will" [Amazon/Kindle]….

ISBN-10: 1544689241

ISBN-13: 978-1544689241

PROLOGUE

"Since 2000 more than 50,000 manufacturing facilities in the U.S. have closed and roughly 50,000 industrial jobs have been lost each month.", Congressman Conyers—and resulting in a massive loss of income to the American economy....

So why isn't the truth on the table—so we can change the dialogue? That is, include that unemployment not only adversely impacts the jobless, <u>*but the bottom line, as well!*</u>

And the sad fact is, folks, is that for US.....US humans are chucked into our economy the same as a desk, or steering wheel—an index to be manipulated by economists—We are just not given that much importance—i.e., we are an item, in the law, to be used and discarded "at will"---

And this did not happen by accident—indeed, since WW II the Koch brothers [a metaphor, and fact, for the 1%] have spent hundreds of millions buying governors and legislators to cement "at will" employment in every state [only Montana limits to probationary employees], and to destroy our labor unions!

Their objective is to have employees *without rights* [a slave by definition—cheap labor]—and the loss of income to the bottom line is blindsided in this mind-set.

The over-arching problem, of course, is a corrupted system—and made infinitely worse by Citizens United-- where our politicians are bought and paid for by the Koch brothers…..[every Republican in Congress, and far too many Democrats….]….

And over-looked is that our economy is only about one species—US, US human beings…..to illustrate, if we were recognized in our economy as we should be our Job Creation would be based on "fix unemployment, and this will fix the market"….rather that our current incompetent, and unworkable "fix the market, and this will fix unemployment"….

A primary thrust in this book, however, is a corollary issue—Job Creation…..which will never be fixed until the American people get a handle on our electoral process—and we again have a seat at the table in creating "JOBS, JOBS, JOBS"—which has been the mantra in every election—with varying degrees of intensity—since the mid-1970's when the world economy underwent a major paradigm shift [more on this throughout]…..and in an odd twist—laid the groundwork for a Trump presidency…..

The doctor can't perform the operation without the proper medical instruments, and the mechanic can't fix the engine without the proper tools….and it is this exact dilemma facing America in creating jobs--going forward in the 21st Century....

Since WW II our Job Creation has been based on the belief: "The market can provide anybody wanting a job, with a job"....but as it has turned out--this is PURE BS....and this model has not resulted in an unemployment [hereafter UE] rate below 3% since 1953!

Leaving millions jobless in its wake, it has resulted in our inner-cities with 60% minority UE, drug economies, and an epidemic of gun violence!

Further, under this model, if the market fails—the jobless are out of luck....

In short, while we have gotten a lot of lip service from politicians over the years—about the millions of jobs they are going to create, if elected—it has always been within the context/assumption that we will have a robust economy....NOT about creating the jobs they claim...i.e., fixing UE....

And thus the electorate's demand for "JOBS, JOBS, JOBS"…..is ignored—with a growing resentment—particularly since the 1980's....and a growing consensus that we are "moving in the wrong direction"....

There is little dispute between economists that as a result of the colliding forces of globalization, technology, automation reaching critical mass in the mid-1970's--the world economy underwent a major paradigm shift--leaving "high and pervasive unemployment in almost every OECD country, since"—

And as a result of automation, alone, we have had excessive high UE over 70% of the time, since 1980 [twice that of preceding years]—in sum, it is Robots, not Mexicans that is the major impact on our Job Creation going forward in the 21st Century….

To come full circle, we can't create the millions of jobs we need to create going forward in our 21 Century market economy—without the proper tools to get the job done!

Our economy, today, is what it is….for instance, robots/automation, alone, are resulting in fewer and fewer jobs—the further we advance into the 21st Century—and yet, our job creation model, today, is still lodged in the 18th Century—with our evolving sabotaged because it is propagandized to be "communism, or socialism, or God forbid "liberal"— i.e., our economy is being suffocated by idiocy!

Unemployment is a *No One Wins* –the jobless lose, civility loses [Ferguson, et al], and the Market loses, to wit:

THE LAW OF DIMINISHED INCOME TO THE MARKET FROM UNEMPLOYMENT [hereafter D/UE LAW]

3% is the zero-sum threshold above which unemployment triggers inflation by diminishing labor training and skills, under-utilizing capital resources, reducing the rate of productivity advance, increasing unit labor costs, reducing the general supply of goods and services--and the loss in income to the Market is compounded exponentially with each percentage point of increase in unemployment, above 3%.

Short Definition:

3% is the zero-sum threshold above which unemployment starts substantially undermining the Market--and the loss in income to the Market is compounded exponentially with each percentage point of increase in unemployment, above 3%.

A few closing comments in the Prologue—As Oscar Wilde averred "The only truly worthless opinion is an unbiased one"—so bias, agreed—but always in the interest in getting at the larger goal—the truth….

Incidentally, I published my first book on my 78th birthday [I am currently 82—so just hang out for the nuggets when I wander…]—and not that I write that fast, or well—the materials were all there for the better part of the past 30 years, give or take, gathering dust—it was just a matter of pulling them together in some order—also, don't believe any book should be over 60 pages, plus/minus— i.e., can be read in the crapper--

two hours, max--lol—but it seems best summed up by a very astute observer [wish I could recall their name to give credit]: Persons who write do so because they have no choice [it is a compulsion, an addiction..]—they become an "author", however, when people start reading what they have written….

Finally, a note to the reader—the papers and letters are not in sequence, and apologize for redundancy [please look for the nuggets…Thx--lol]—also, if you are a "typo-wonk"—are more concerned with sentence structure, etc., than content—you probably won't like my writing—and you will find a wayward capital letter, here and there, and appearing out of place and used for emphasis—or a missing page…Hey, I'm and Indie….I chalk most up to editorial license and tongue-in-cheek, self-effacing humor—so apologies, here—[I seriously support: Take what you do seriously, but never yourself….]….

Just look for content, please….THX

CHAPTER ONE

Please Forward To: Stephen Schwarzman, Blackstone CEO

The mantra in the 2016 election was "JOBS, JOBS, JOBS"—indeed, given automation, alone, we have had a growing drumbeat by the electorate for jobs, since 1980—and in spite of the "legal authorization" in Humphrey-Hawkins [1978]—which would have limited our unemployment [hereafter UE] rate in America to 3%, permanently!

And the mind-shattering question, today is: "WHY DID WE LET FLINT ROT INTO DECAY: Ushering In A Trump Presidency?" [Amazon/Kindle]—i.e., why did we stand on one foot and then the other and let Flint/the Rust Belt rot into decay when we had the legal authority, on the books, to prevent it?

For clarity re the above...Humphrey-Hawkins is brilliant, ahead of its time—more valuable today, and with each passing year in the 21st Century—and incredibly misunderstood....

1] Rather than being a liberal, bleeding heart wet dream, it is in fact Pro-Market—and given "The Age of Robots", alone, it is INDISPENSIBLE to the

EFFECTIVE functioning of our 21st Century market economy. See: The D/UE LAW [herein]....

2] And, rather than the cost of implementation being prohibitive [the propaganda used to sabotage its enforcement]—implementation is deficit-neutral—i.e., we can reduce our UE rate to 3%, tomorrow—and it will not add dime to our deficit—for instance, with the passage of deficit-neutral HR 1000 [in Committee], or passage of THE NEIGHBOR-TO-NEIGHBOR JOB CREATION ACT [NTN, Amazon/Kindle]: A federally-mandated Social Insurance, owned by our employed, to provide a fund to hire/train our unemployed. Jobs beget jobs, and for a modest 4% of salary policy cost we can create more "private-sector" jobs in 6 months, than HR 2847 [the HIRE Act] in 6 years.

3] And the most extreme case of it being misunderstood, it cost President Carter his re-election because he did not demand, rather than ignore, enforcement of this law----which he signed....i.e., had Carter enforced the "legal authorization" in this law, and, in fact, reduced our UE rate to "3%" as provided for in the law—there is no way he would have lost the election to Reagan.......

Ref: FULL EMPLOYMENT IS A PRO-MARKET CONCEPT, Amazon/Kindle

Jim Green, Democrat opponent to Lamar Smith, Congress, 2000

CHAPTER TWO

President Obama/Presidential Innovation Fellows:

Since WW II our single method of Job Creation in America has been based on the belief/propaganda that "The market can provide anybody wanting a job, with a job"......[problem is—IT IS PURE BS]....

And when it didn't work--we pretended it did, and drifted into Santa Clause-like wishful thinking—asserting "it is the American way", or "God's will"—or some such lie we told ourselves--as rational Job Creation, in a changing world, drifted further and further away.....

For instance, this method of Job Creation has not resulted in a UE rate below 3% since 1953, but we limped along—terrorized by McCarthyism, and leaving millions jobless—and by the mid-1970's the colliding forces of globalization, automation, technology reached critical mass, resulting in a cosmic shift in the world economy—with subsequent "High and persistent unemployment pervasive throughout the OECD since the mid-1970's", according to Dr. William F. Mitchell, and every credible economist.

And, going forward the data got even more grim—i.e., since 1980 we have had excessive UE 70% of the time [twice that of preceding years], and by the Crash of

2008—8 million were rendered jobless—[and in spite of an extremely anemic recovery we inched down from 10% to 5% UE, inexplicably still relying on the above method]—--

And with the result that by the September 2016 DOL Jobs Report, we still have 8 million Americans looking for work, that can't find any…..and in an economy limping along on a flat tire—as a direct result of high UE, and a Republican Congress determined to sabotage America—for political reasons--

The lesson is: Our choices are adapt and change in a world that is changing—whether we like it or not—or be forced to create a Police State to hold in place antiquated and unworkable laws and policies [in this case re our Job Creation]—and sadly, America has opted for the latter—and we need look no further than the police marching in lock-step in Charlotte, this past week, as proof!

The flaw in all of this is based on simple common sense: "The mechanic can't fix the engine without the proper tools"—and when Jobs, Jobs, Jobs is the major mantra in this election—fixing unemployment is hopeless so long as we insist on a method of Job Creation—THAT DOESN'T WORK!

Proposed Solutions: HR 1000, and FULL EMPLOYMENT IS A PRO-MARKET CONCEPT, Amazon

Jim Green, Democrat opponent to Lamar Smith, 2000

Thank you for contacting the White House!

CHAPTER THREE

President Obama/Council of Economic Advisers:

In an age when Americans appear to be divided right down the middle—and a war of words--perhaps we need to step back and take stock:

Capitalism is ideal in producing and selling corn flakes and cars—It doesn't work in solving "social problems" such as unemployment and our healthcare....

And when we have tried "privatization" to solve our social problems—it has been a disaster:

Specifically, essential programs have been cut—such as the elimination of text books from the Job Corps education program—to increase profits, and cronyism has run rampant—

And in our "for profit" healthcare system, billions of dollars are siphoned away from the premiums we send in—and do not go to the healthcare of ANYONE—but rather is used to pay for lobbyists, to make the CEO's filthy rich—and spent on propaganda ads to keep it that way!

Additionally, President Obama had a weapon in 2009, not available to FDR: Were it not for the $800 billion in Social Security Insurance moneys percolating up through our economy annually, ie., in 2008—we would not be talking about having narrowly averted another Great Depression—We would be buried in one!

The truth is, we have a blended economic system—and the two components are, in fact, indispensable to each other:

Social Insurance is a vital ingredient in building a vibrant and decent society—And, invent a better widget, sell the company for a million bucks, and retire in Florida [capitalism]—is as well a vital ingredient in building a vibrant and decent society.

So why do we have this war of words pitting the two against each other—rather than educating the American people regarding the indispensable symbiotic relationship they have to each other?

Were it not for the $2 trillion + Washington infuses back into the economy annually—capitalism would fold in a NY Second!

And yet, most Republicans ask God in their prayers at night to be protected from communists, or socialists, or even worse "liberals"—[i.e., monsters under their bed] with "liberal" henceforth to be replaced with the word "Christian"…..

Regarding "unemployment" [hereafter UE]—it is essential that we evolve, and given "automation", alone, in our 21st Century economy we need to look upon UE the same as we look upon Cancer, Polio, or AIDS, as a ubiquious disease—a menace to society, in need of eradication….via [15 USC § 3101]—which would restrict our UE to 3%, permanently!

Jim Green, Democrat candidate for Congress, 2000

CHAPTER FOUR

RE: Press Conference 11/14/12

Mr. F. Michael Kelleher,
Special Assistant to the President
Director of Presidential Correspondence

President Obama/Fellow Democrats:

The most profound statement in "The Audacity of Hope" is "most [Americans] thought that anybody willing to work should be able to find a job…."…. according to a recent Zogby poll "86% of Americans" believe this….

And yet, save for a lone member of Congress—Representative Conyers [HR 1000, in Committee]—Washington does not have any legislation on the table that is specifically directed at responding to this mind-set on the part of the American people--

This mind-set bears repeating:

Most Americans believe that anybody willing to work, should be able to find a job—We are a democracy—so why is this not a reality? —And, particularly when it is a Pro-Market solution? The market thrives when we have a robust, employed, consuming workforce--

There are two distinct paths to job creation, in America—and in spite of its incompetence in creating jobs, Washington keeps insisting on taking the path that it is ONLY the "market" that can create jobs [rather than being a component in a blended solution]—and in spite of the fact that if the market fails—the unemployed are out of luck!

And this also underscores why it is the wrong path to follow:

We are trying to solve a complex "social" problem with a highly unstable entity—the market—rather than looking at unemployment [which demands a stable solution] as a "stand alone" social problem—and which we, as a society, have an absolute responsibility to address—the other path---

And as the American people said loud and clear in "Audacity….".. We want to address! It is Washington that isn't listening! In short, Washington has been pursuing: Fix the economy, and employment will follow—when exactly the opposite is true—fix unemployment and this will in turn fix the economy--

In listening to the American people the following is proposed: The Neighbor-To-Neighbor Job Creation Act—a federally mandated, Social Insurance—owned by our employed, to provide a fund to hire/train our unemployed. And the infrastructure is in place via FICA.

For a modest policy cost of 4% of salary we can reduce our unemployment rate to 3% within one year of passage—and as "authorized" in 15 USC § 3101. For more detail please see www.Inclusivism.org

Jim Green, Democrat candidate for Congress, 2000

CHAPTER FIVE

FUNDING OUR INFRASTRUCTURE JOBS

Senator Schumer, to fund the infrastructure jobs, which Trump supports, please consider THE NEIGHBOR-TO-NEIGHBOR JOB CREATION ACT [hereafter NTN, Amazon/Kindle]. It is both Pro-Market, and deficit-neutral…i.e., a federally mandated Social Insurance, held by our employed, to provide a fund to hire/train our unemployed. Jobs beget jobs, and for a modest 4% of salary policy cost we will create more "private-sector" jobs in 6 months, than HR 2847 in 6 years—and the funding negates the Republican's effort to sabotage the repairs every reasonable person agrees are urgent….and Trump is onboard!

Best regards,

Jim Green, Democrat candidate for Congress, Dist 21, TX, 2000

Thank you for contacting Senator Schumer

CHAPTER SIX

POSTED: April 18, 2014

President Obama/Council of Economic Advisers:

The field of Economics is awash in graphs and tables—to tell us the health or ill of our economy, but none, nada which warn us of the danger of how unemployment impacts the bottom line.

High Unemployment [6.7%]/Sluggish Recovery is not a non-sequitur. Our manufacturing is disappearing because people do not buy stuff when they are jobless. The prism this problem is currently being looked through has something to do with our laws –[the oligarchy] regarding "employees" in America—which still have one foot on the plantation—

As a result of this anachronistic mind-set the Republicans blather on in magical thinking—with the promise that if we cut taxes for the 1%, they will create jobs [and not spend this windfall on a bigger yacht—they promise--wink, wink]; and the Democrats stand on one foot and then the other—as we inch along--waiting on the Market to fix our unemployment crisis—and if the Market fails, the unemployed are out of luck!

The larger point being: We need to change the

dialogue—we need to change the message. We need to start showing how unemployment cuts into corporate profits.

We currently have the "legal authorization", on the books, to limit our unemployment to 3% [15 USC § 3101]--i.e., at no time should our unemployment exceed 3%--but given the mind-set in Washington, today, it might as well be written in Greek. Congressman Conyer's deficit-neutral, Pro-Market HR 1000 never got out of Committee, while it should be voted on today—given our highest priority—and while unlikely, the Republicans might get on board if we shifted the emphasis.

This is a case where the American people are way ahead of Washington…86 % believe that "anybody wanting to work should be able to find a job"—i.e., 15 USC § 3101 has solid political support--Washington just isn't listening.

Given "automation" alone, an expanding and contracting public workforce is an INDISPENSABLE component to the EFFECTIVE functioning of our 21st Century economy—and we need to introduce into our dialogue, IMHO:

"3% is the zero-sum threshold above which unemployment starts undermining the Market--and the loss in income to the Market is compounded exponentially with each percentage point of increase in unemployment, above 3%".

FULL EMPLOYMENT IS A PRO-MARKET CONCEPT, Amazon

Jim Green, Democrat opponent to Lamar Smith, Congress, 2000

CHAPTER SEVEN

PLEASE FORWARD TO: Dr. Charles Wheelan RE: BOOK TV 5-1-16—re "Naked Money"--In the discussion of your book you noted the dual mandate for the FED, i.e., "protecting the purchasing power of the dollar and also to maintain full employment"—as part of this you quoted Ben Bernanke—and I took from this, also current accepted economic theory [written in stone] that "The only way to maximize full employment is by making sure there isn't any inflation or deflation." My purpose in writing is to challenge that our economists have this wrong—in seeking a way to fix unemployment [hereafter UE]--it is an error to make "employment" an index in our economic system—and I think we started down this erroneous path because we are looking through the prism—i.e., we are still trying to make work the propaganda by the plutocracy/oligarchy, since WW II, that "the market can provide anybody wanting a job, with a job"—and excuse the French but this is pure BS—the only year since WW II that this Job Creation methodology has resulted in a UE rate below 3% was 1953—leaving millions jobless in its wake—and this mind-set has turned our inner-cities into war zones, with drug economies, and an epidemic of gun violence. Indeed, we need look no further than Flint to understand the devastation to communities caused by UE. In short, to fix we need to start looking at UE as a "social" problem—much the same as we look at a pandemic—which we, as the larger society, attack directly--rather than depending on outside factors, or wishful thinking to solve, and the FED, to meet its mandate, needs to look for a solution through this prism. I understand you may disagree but think you will find of interest **FULL EMPLOYMENT IS A PRO-MARKET CONCEPT, and THE CASE FOR WORK BEING A LEGAL RIGHT, Amazon/Kindle**

Jim Green, candidate for Congress, 2000

Bio: http://www.amazon.com/James-L.-Jim-Green/e/B001KHZIMM/ref=ntt_dp_epwbk_0

CHAPTER EIGHT

Over the past several decades observing...and often finding what we are doing a puzzlement [such as pretending the 800 Carrier jobs is anything other than a political gimmick—when we need to create 200,000 jobs a month just to keep up with our birthrate] but through the BS, I formulated some solutions to our social problems that I assert will actually work—and being a capitalist, have identified as "Neo-Capitalism". To distinguish from other programs, and to identify, coined the name: ECONOMIC INCLUSIVISM, and have a book on Amazon/Kindle. Since 1996, I have had a web page on the internet: www.Inclusivism.org My thinking has evolved over the years, and have zeroed in on Job Creation—I believe our solution to unemployment to be the most important issue facing America going forward in the 21 Century—but posting, here, are my proposed solutions, defined as Economic Inclusivism:

ECONOMIC INCLUSIVISM: Neo-Capitalism--A 21st Century Solution

[Social/Prison Reforms]

1) We need to re-classify all crime in the future as violent or non-violent, and discard the archaic terms felony and misdemeanor. The word felony has been implanted in the public's mind to mean "armed and

dangerous", and yet over 70% of our prison inmates (all felons) are in prison for non-violent offenses. As a result, the term "felony" is distracting us from addressing the real problem....the violent offender.

2) We need a much greater use of "Shock" Incarceration (A sentencing alternative I authored in the 1960's); a greater use of fines, restitution, and probation (both civil and criminal), in lieu of incarceration, and fines paid directly to victims instead of the state all as part of an expanded menu of sentencing alternatives. [We have 5% of the world's population, and 25% of all prison inmates on earth, in our prisons! If we had the same proportion of inmates to general population as the rest of the civilized world, we would have 400,000 persons incarcerated, not 2,200,000, as we do at present! And yet our PR is that we are the most free country in the world? We daily turn non-violent persons into violent career criminals, with over 99% released back into society, making life in America MORE dangerous, not less! And the grizzly stabbing death, in Illinois, of 8 and 9 year old girls, on Mother's Day, 2005, by a recently released inmate, is a textbook example of this inept approach…..when on earth are we going to accept that to whatever degree....we are also part of the problem? Prison should be a last resort, not first!] We can correct this by mandating that our legislatures return to the pre-1988 (pre the Willie Horton ad) standard: For every $1 budgeted for prisons, $5 MUST be budgeted for the education of our children. This appx ratio was not set by statute, but rather by tradition and common sense. At present, we budget more for prisons than educating

our youth, and were not becoming a police state?

3) We need to create Federal Regional Diagnostic and Treatment Centers, for the diagnosis and treatment of the violent offender. We have learned a great deal about violent behavior in recent years (see www.brainplace.com), and yet we do not have a cohesive or concerted national program or policy in America for dealing with this national epidemic and disgrace. The sheer numbers of homicides by handguns, alone, tells the whole story: Canada 151, Australia 57, Germany 373, Japan 19, England and Wales 54, the United States 11,789! When we add in all deaths by guns, including the fact that 9 children are killed by guns everyday in America, our gun violence escalates to a staggering 28,663! Also, we need to allow for voluntary admissions to these Centers, to prevent juvenile and family violence. It is essential that we seek out "problem-solving", not "punishment" oriented solutions, which actually exacerbate crime.

4) We need to pick-up the lead taken by England, in treating drug addiction as a "medical" rather than a "criminal" problem, so that we can EFFECTIVELY curb drug-related crime, and keep drugs out of the hands of our youth. To demonstrate how specious our thinking has become in this area, alcohol and tobacco kill ten of thousands of persons annually, and yet these drugs are not classified as "dangerous". The tiny handful of persons with "addictive personalities" has totally shaped our drug policies while "addiction", in all of its forms, can only EFFECTIVELY be treated with a medical solution. We have wasted billions on

interdiction, and yet, youth drug abuse is actually increasing.

[Economic Reforms]

5) To address our insidious practice of "exclusion", Congress must acknowledge a citizen's legal right to work (1), as enacted by Congress in "The Full Employment Act of 1946", and as outlined in the Democratic National Platform position asserting "Opportunity to every American". The right to work and be a productive member of one's society is also a human right. Accordingly, we must ratify the following constitutional amendment: "Work shall hereafter be the legal right of every citizen, and Congress shall, except for retirement/disability programs under federal jurisdiction, make no laws which will abridge the right of any citizen of legal age, to work and be a productive citizen." [Our lapse in enlightenment regarding this urgently needed systemic change -- believed by the ignorant and uninformed to be "communism" -- combined with some really peculiar notions about guns, is the cause for almost all violent crime in America. This is a "practical" rather than a "liberal" solution in our 21st Century economy, a point totally lost on ideologues. This is not a "safety net" (the conservative propaganda buzz term to undermine "social" programs), this is recognizing within each of us a "human right". The distinction is as different as night and day. Further, rather than being a wildly radical idea, a recent Zogby poll found that "86% of Americans think the government should provide a job to anyone who wants one", according to the April 4,

2005 issue of The Nation. Economic Inclusivism, however, does not ask that the government provide a job, but rather recognizes within each citizen the legal right to work and be a prouctive member of the society, as a HUMAN RIGHT. Also, For clarity, I am a capitalist. I support limited interference on the part of government in the free enterprise system, and find the ownership of "business", or a government controlled economy, as currently incorporated in both socialism and communism, to be patently absurd. We will always have government controls so that we have safe food, and medicine, etc., and we rightfully should have, that is separate and apart from the government doing, what a free enterprise business can do better. I would vehemently disagree that our recognition within each citizen a "human right" to work and be a productive citizen to be an interference with the free enterprise system, and it would have more of a psychological impact on the individual, than an economic impact on the economy, as it currently exists. A person wishing to become a doctor, will still become a doctor, or a CEO, or bartender, whatever…..people do what is most compatible with their nature and talents and Economic Inclusuvism would not change that. Indeed, it in some cases it would provide a greater assist in their reaching their goal, than is currently available, and it is much more efficient in utilizing our greatest resource: humans, that our current system. Most importantly, it is the right thing to do].

6) To ensure enforcement/fund this legal right, Congress would create a privately owned, federally mandated, Social Insurance, with limited ownership by

each person who works, which would provide work/training to any citizen who applies. Work could include: Child care for low income working families, building a high-speed rail system, the urgent need outlined by the NEA for School Modernization, the creation of Federal Regional Diagnostic and Treatment Centers for the diagnosis and treatment of the violent offender [HINT: convert our excessive new prisons into said Centers], repairing our rotting infrastructure (the list of social benefits is endless). As owners of this plan, each worker would vote on proposed national projects and dividends would be paid annually from unused funds. A projected cost of 8% would be less than the worker currently pays for welfare. [Like Social Security and military retirement moneys, Economic Inclusivism would STRENGTHEN, not weaken the business community....these steps are necessary to preserve, not harm capitalism in a rapidly changing economy...Bill Gates became the richest man in the world because of these monies percolating through the economy....If W (and the wacko Neo-Con ideas) was the president in the 30's, instead of FDR, Bill Gates would be on the street with a "Will work for food" signs.....and further this will prevent our further movement down the erroneous path towards communism or towards the other extreme, fascism (our current movement), both of which require a dictator, and the wholesale loss of our civil liberties, to hold the government in place.]

7) Since this program of "inclusion" would address 95% of our social ills (crime, welfare, drugs, etc., and exacerbated in many cases by inept Band-Aid

programs), the federal budget could be greatly reduced and our current Federal Income Tax would be replaced with a National Sales Tax, value-added tax, a national lottery, or some combination of taxes other than our current Federal Income Tax. We currently spend 26 billion annually for the Internal Revenue Service, and corporations and individuals spend trillions trying to get around the Tax Code, all of which is passed on to us, the consumer, in the higher cost of consumer goods.

7a)A Universal Healthcare System is an essential ingredient of a sane society!

CHAPTER NINE

The following email, in the Congressional Record, from Newsmax, is being brought front and center because it underscores that SUPPLY-SIDE REFRIED is a SCAM by Trump/Republicans to STEAL from the American people...to pander to KB GREED, and as payback for donations......while sending the bill to pay for their tax cuts for the wealthy to our grandchildren to pay!

"Millionaires Tell Congress: Raise Our Taxes"

"A well-heeled group calling itself the Patriotic Millionaires for Fiscal Strength is planning to lobby Capitol Hill on Wednesday with an unusual request: "Tax me."

" With the supercommittee's Thanksgiving-eve deadline less than two weeks away, members of Patriotic Millionaires — open only to people with incomes of $1 million and higher — plan to testify at a hearing on jobs and taxes, then meet with supercommittee members and their staffs, other Congressional leaders and lawmakers from the Tea Party Caucus.

"It will take all patriotic Americans working together to fix the problems irresponsible politicians caused by cutting taxes for millionaires at the same time they put two wars on the nation's credit card," insists Erica Payne of Patriotic Millionaires. "We need to pay for the choices we make. These Patriotic Millionaires are willing to do that. On Wednesday, we will ask our elected officials if they are willing to do the same."

"They are willing to pay more in taxes because the sacrifice is both an ethical and patriotic decision," according to a group statement. "It is made in the hopes of allowing the United States to continue to be a leader economically, politically, and morally. Any deal reached by the super committee that does not ask millionaires to pay their fair share should be vetoed."

"Initially formed to urge President Barack Obama to let the Bush-era tax cuts expire for people making more than $1 million a year, membership has now swelled to 200, and includes more than a dozen current and former Google employees; actress Edie Falco ("The Sopranos"); the founders of Esprit, the Princeton Review, and Ask.com; philanthropist Michael Steinhardt; economist Nouriel Roubini; financial guru Andrew Tobias; top executives from Warburg, Pincus; and filmmaker Abigail Disney.

"An outpouring of public support encouraged them to continue their fight," the group says, citing the following:

- Only 375,000 Americans have incomes of over $1 million.

- Between 1979 and 2007, incomes for the wealthiest 1 percent of Americans rose by 281 percent.
- During the Great Depression, millionaires had a top marginal tax rate of 68 percent.
- In 1963 millionaires had a top marginal tax rate of 91 percent.
- In 1976 millionaires had a top marginal tax rate of 70 percent.
- Today, millionaires have a top marginal tax rate of 35 percent.
- Reducing the income tax on top earners is one of the most inefficient ways to grow the economy, according to the Congressional Budget Office.
- 44 percent of Congress people are millionaires.

The Bush tax cuts were never meant to be permanent, and letting them expire for the top 2 percent would pay down the debt by $700 billion over the next 10 years."

CHAPTER TEN

Mr. David Stockman…[Reagan OMB Director] re interview with Ali Velshi---MSNBC—3/1/17….First, let me say that we have far more work that needs to be done in America, than we have persons to fill these jobs….and with that in mind, WHY, in God's name—when it comes to Job Creation in America—are our policy makers entrenched in the belief that "the market can provide anybody wanting a job, with a job"?—[it is pure BS]—and evident by the data—this model, which has driven our Job Creation since WW II, has not resulted in an unemployment [hereafter UE] rate below 3% since 1953! Leaving millions jobless in its wake, this mind-set for Job Creation has resulted in our inner-cities with 60% minority UE, drug economies, and an epidemic of gun violence!

I am aware that we are on a different sheet of music [I have always thought Supply-Side was Voodoo, or worse—sorry]—but I respect your honesty when you saw its flaws—and you spoke up even then as I recall—and appreciate your depth in explaining complex economic issues.

My primary reason for writing regards how we create jobs in our 21st Century market economy—[the most critical economic issue facing America, today--IMHO] and agree with your observation that Trumps's speech was "fiscally irresponsible"—he claims he will create "millions of jobs"—but he has ZERO job creation programs to accomplish this!

Trump, the Republican agenda, today, is an "IF" job creation program, based on "wishful thinking" [and in which, if the market fails, the jobless are out of luck!]—but cutting to the chase—since 1980, we have had a growing drumbeat from the electorate for JOBS, JOBS, JOBS—and given automation, alone, the problem becomes more pronounced with each passing year in our 21st Century market economy.

And I will add something, here, which I suspect you may vehemently disagree….that Humphrey-Hawkins [hereafter HH--15 USC § 3101] is pure genius….perhaps inadvertently, it correctly anticipated our 21st Century market economy—it is a Pro-Market solution in this economy—people do not buy what we manufacture when they are jobless--indeed, why we stood on one foot and then the other and let Flint/the Rust Belt rot into decay—[and created the breeding ground for a Trump presidency!]--when we had the "legal authorization" to limit our UE rate to 3%--permanently, from 1978 on—escapes me!

To tie this together—jobs beget jobs and had we enforced HH—[rather than pushed it under the rug almost from the minute Carter signed it] this method of Job Creation would have resulted in more "private-sector" jobs in 6 months, today, than HR 2847 [the HIRE Act], in 6 years!

Finally, I don't know if you are familiar with HR 1000 [21st Century HH], but it is a Pro-Market, deficit-neutral method to create the "millions of jobs"....both Trump and Hillary promised—and in the same genre is: THE NEIGHBOR-TO-NEIGHBOR JOB CREATION ACT [NTN--Amazon/Kindle]: A federally mandated Social Insurance, held by our employed, to provide a fund to hire/train our UE—and triggered anytime our UE rate rises above 3%, per HH. For a modest 4% of salary policy cost we can create the "millions of jobs" Trump has promised....[see D/UE Law in NTN, above]....

My over-arching point is that fixing UE is critical in addressing every other economic factor—and absent fixing UE causes all other solutions to fall short—in sum—"fix unemployment, and this will fix the market"—rather than our current incompetent "fix the market, and this will fix UE"....

Ref: FULL EMPLOYMENT IS A PRO-MARKET CONCEPT, and SUPPLY-SIDE REFRIED Amazon/Kindle

Best regards,

Jim Green, Democrat opponent to Lamar Smith, Congress, 2000

CHAPTER ELEVEN

President Obama/Council of Economic Advisers/Presidential Innovation Fellows:

WE NEED TO CHANGE THE DIALOGUE....

There is universal agreement by every politician in the 2016 election on our need for "Jobs, Jobs, Jobs"--but we cannot create jobs in the absence of a viable Job Creation methodology—and to change our current antiquated/unworkable method of Job Creation [that the market can provide everybody with work---which has not created an unemployment rate below 3% since 1953, with a resulting epidemic of gun violence in our inner-cities]—

AND, to make this urgently needed change--WE need to change the dialogue—Since WW II our focus on the need for Job Creation has been based on the adverse impact on the individual—and not to diminish this in the slightest, but the other side of this coin is the devastation caused to the MARKET, as a result of unemployment—people do not buy what we manufacture when they are jobless—Unemployment is a NO ONE WINS: The jobless lose, civility loses [Ferguson, etc.], and the MARKET loses, to wit:

OUR SLUGGISH ECONOMY RESULTING FROM THE LAW OF DIMINISHED INCOME TO THE MARKET FROM UNEMPLOYMENT [hereafter D/UE LAW]

3% is the zero-sum threshold above which unemployment triggers inflation by diminishing labor training and skills, under-utilizing capital resources, reducing the rate of productivity advance, increasing unit labor costs, reducing the general supply of goods and services--and the loss in income to the Market is compounded exponentially with each percentage point of increase in unemployment, above 3%.

The bottom line is, to get the change EVERYONE agrees we urgently need—we need to change the dialogue—we need to change the emphasis—and get the Koch bros [a metaphor for the 1%]—to look at the income the market is losing because of their "one foot on the plantation" mind-set----not saying this will be easy---i.e, to engage the 1% in a solution that will benefit EVERYONE—to point out how UE adversely impacts the bottom line….but it is unlikely this change will ever come about until we change the dialogue, and the Koch bros see Humphrey-Hawkins for what it actually is: A Pro-Market solution in our 21st Century market economy.

Ref: HR 1000 [in Committee], THE NEIGHBOR-TO-NEIGHBOR JOB CREATION ACT [NTN], IT IS IMPOSSIBLE TO BE A CHRISTIAN, AND VOTE REPUBLICAN, Amazon/Kindle

Jim Green, Democrat opponent to Lamar Smith, Congress, 2000

Thank you for contacting the White House!

CHAPTER TWELVE

Fareed Zakaria: Re your interview with President Obama—why is Job Creation not front and center in these discussions [in this election]—i.e., the method by which we create jobs/eliminate unemployment [hereafter UE]? We can't have Jobs, Jobs, Jobs without a healthy Job Creation policy! Since WW II, policy driving our Job Creation in America has been based on the belief/propaganda [lie] that "The market can provide anybody wanting a job, with a job"—it is the reason we stood on one foot and then the other as we inched downward—waiting on the market to correct itself—with the result of an extremely anemic 5% from our UE rate since 2009—and leaving 20 millions still underemployed/unemployed!

Also, in every recession since WW II we have had a rapid recovery—a "V" shaped recovery—while this has been an "L" shaped recovery—almost flat lined—and singularly because we have a Job Creation method that doesn't work! For instance, the above policy has not resulted in a UE rate below 3% since 1953—leaving millions jobless in its wake, and turned our inner-cities into war zones with an epidemic of gun violence! In short, this is the most dangerous policy facing America today! And, the bottom line is that unemployment is a NO ONE WINS…..the jobless lose, civility loses [Ferguson, etc.,], and the MARKET LOSES, to wit:

OUR SLUGGISH RECOVERY/ECONOMY RESULTNG FROM THE LAW OF DIMINISHED INCOME TO THE MARKET FROM UNEMPLOYMENT [hereafter D/UE LAW]

Short Definition:

3% is the zero-sum threshold above which unemployment starts substantially undermining the Market--and the loss in income to the Market is compounded exponentially with each percentage point of increase in unemployment, above 3%.

Ref: FULL EMPLOYMENT IS A PRO-MARKET CONCEPT, Amazon/Kindle

Jim Green, Democrat opponent to Lamar Smith, Congress, 2000

Thank you for contacting the White House!

CHAPTER THIRTEEN

To Whom It May Concern:

Noli Tangere: Latin for "Do Not Touch" it is the warning from the 1% to the politicians--the 1% have spent tens of millions buying since WW II—to not touch Job Creation in America—i.e., the warning that Job Creation in America is our province and sealed with the propaganda/lie that "the market can provide anybody wanting a job, with a job"—it is PURE BS…..and only ONCE since WW II has this resulted in an unemployment [hereafter UE] rate below 3%--in 1953—leaving millions jobless in its wake—and it turned Flint into a war zone, with 60% minority UE, a drug economy, and an epidemic of gun violent.

The point is we don't need look any further than Flint, as proof, to understand the destruction caused to a community by UE—and yet, we as the larger society, don't have the means to solve the problem because the 1%, up to now, have bought our elections and has prevented Washington from fixing our unemployment crisis!

The late Peter Drucker advocated for CEO salaries being limited to 20 times that of the lowest paid employee [the Swiss recently had on the ballot 12 times]— but it is argued that a brain-drain would occur if we didn't leave this to the market to set CEO salaries—

And whether or not this is true— WHY on earth do our policy makers persist in the anachronistic BELIEF that the market can provide anybody wanting a job, with a job [untrue since the 1950's]--and given automation, alone--an expanding and contracting public workforce is an INDISPENSABLE component to the EFFECTIVE functioning of our modern market economy…..

CHAPTER FOURTEEN

Editor: NY TIMES

WILL POLITICS NEVER CHANGE?

A Republican candidate for president said "On next January 20, there will begin in Washington, the biggest unraveling, unsnarling, untangling operation in our nation's history."

But before Republican ideologues say "right on" regarding their belief in unraveling President Obama's administration— this was from a speech by Republican candidate Tom Dewey, and directed at President Truman, in 1948!

Given the political rhetoric you would think President Truman [and President Obama] couldn't even tie their own shoes— albeit, President Truman had ended WWII [while President Obama has rescued America from another Great Depression, and got bin Laden, etc., etc.,].

And other parallels between these two elections are even more striking. For instance, Truman was outraged by what he called a "Do nothing Congress"— and he went on to warn the electorate that "The country cannot afford another Republican Congress." No informed American will dispute that, today....

The most startling parallel, however, is when Truman said of the Republican Congress on a stump speech "It is a sad tale of the sell out of the American people to these gluttons of privilege— these cold men who skim the cream from our natural resources to satisfy their own greed."

This could have been said yesterday, and yet, it was said by President Truman 68 years ago!

Finally, President Truman offered some words of wisdom to the American electorate on the danger of returning our government back to the Republicans [as true today, as then] "I'm just waking you up to the fact that this is YOUR fight— and YOU are going to be the loser [if you return the White House back to the Republicans]."

And, as every student of History knows, and in spite of the inexcusable headline error by the Chicago Tribune "DEWEY DEFEATS TRUMAN"— President Truman did win—and kept the White House where it belongs— with a Democrat!

Ref: IT IS IMPOSSIBLE TO BE A CHRISTIAN, AND VOTE REPUBLICAN, Amazon/Kindle

Jim Green, Democrat opponent to Lamar Smith, Congress, 2000

CHAPTER FIFTEEN

President Obama/Council of Economic Advisers:

The most important lesson to be learned from our sluggish recovery is that the world has changed, and to keep pace it is imperative that we change how we create jobs.

Historically, every recession since WW II has been followed by a strong recovery--and every credible economic experts agrees that our inability, today, to create jobs [our high unemployment] has been central in our resulting sluggish recovery—

And the impact on the elderly has been the most evident, and one of the hardest hit....

In 2010, and for the first time since 1975 when the Cost of Living Adjustment [COLA] rate was created by law, to protect our elderly and disabled from pernicious inflation—the COLA in 2010 was "0.0"—

There was a COLA adjustment in EVERY previous year....but it didn't stop there and COLA was again flat-lined at "0.0" in 2011, and again in 2016----while in the same time frame we had a cumulative 12.7% increase in inflation in the same almost 8 years.

And while we can all celebrate the turnaround after the Republicans trashed our economy in 2008--it is evident by COLA, alone, that we have been in an extremely anemic recovery—

The bottom line, however, is the correlation between: "High Unemployment & Sluggish Recovery/Economy" —the former causing the latter.

Since WW II, and the [FULL] EMPLOYMENT ACT OF 1946 [to create jobs for our returning troops], we have had two distinct paths to Job Creation in America:

1] The belief/propaganda [lie] that the market can create all the jobs we need, and….

2] Outlined in pro-market, deficit-neutral Humphrey-Hawkins [hereafter HH] in 1978—that would trigger Job Creation from a "reservoir of public employees" anytime our UE rate rises above "3%"…..[currently HR 1000, in Committee].

The plutocracy/oligarchy hated [didn't understand] HH, however, and with hundreds of millions to buy our elections Washington pretty much hated HH too…..i.e., its "legal authorization" has never been enforced….

And evident by our current recovery—with President Obama ill-advised by his Council of Economic Advisers—i.e., given "automation" alone, eliminating jobs it is evident we are long over-due in changing course—we are long over-due in enforcing the "legal authorization" in HH.

Ref: FULL EMPLOYMNET IS A PRO-MARKET CONCEPT, Amazon/Kindle

Jim Green, Democrat opponent to Lamar Smith, Congress, 2000

CHAPTER SIXTEEN

POSTINGS ON FACEBOOK:

Auto insurance is mandatory in almost every state [every country]—we don't want our highways clogged with uninsured drivers—and also having everyone covered drives the cost down. The same principle applies to the ACA—if only the ill, like only bad drivers, signed up—the insurance would collapse for everyone—So why did Trump/the Republicans gut the mandatory requirements in their "so called" healthcare bill—and also, inexplicably, include a massive tax cut for the 1%--in their replacement bill? Let's face it folks, because they are INSUFFERABLE JERKS! And: IT IS IMPOSSIBLE TO BE A CHRISTIAN, AND VOTE REPUBLICAN, and SUPPLY-SIDE REFRIED, Amazon/Kindle

Re: CNN, program the BELIEVER…3/5/17….We so underestimate the power of "belief"—and evident by the program, not always for good….but this is not limited to marginal religions, and can be equally pernicious in America, today. For instance, our mode of job creation since WW II….the BELIEF that "the market can provide anybody wanting a job, with a job"—it is PURE BS….and has not resulted in an unemployment rate below 3% since 1953—leaving millions jobless in its wake, since, and resulted in our epidemic of gun violence! And yet, Trump, as well as every Republican in Congress lie to the American people by asserting this "belief", as if it were "fact"—by asserting that a massive tax cut for the 1% WILL result in jobs---when, in fact, it is PURE CHANCE, at best, and if the market fails the jobless are out of luck! In short, saying this SCAM will create jobs is a LIE….and like "Trumpcare", a FRAUD to rip-off the American people and send the bill to pay for the massive tax cuts for the 1%, to our grandchildren to pay! ! Ref: "SUPPLY-SIDE REFRIED: The Trump/Republican Scam To Rob Americans Blind, Again!", Amazon/Kindle

CHAPTER SEVENTEEN

President Obama/Council of Economic Advisers:

THE HISTORY OF HUMPHREY-HAWKINS

The historic March On Washington, and Dr. King's "I had a dream" speech, in 1963, was a march for JOBS.

At that time, and to this day, our job creation in America has been based on the premise that "the market can provide anybody wanting a job, with a job—

And yet, only ONCE since WW II has this method of job creation resulted in an unemployment rate below 3%--in 1953—leaving millions jobless in its wake.

Following Dr. Kings death in 1968, civil rights leaders, including Jesse Jackson, annually marched on Dr. King's birthday for legislation that would address our pervasive unemployment in America.

Their demand was not without legal foundation. In 1946, President Truman signed into law the [FULL] EMPLOYMENT ACT OF 1946, to provide employment for our troops returning from WW II.

The 1%, however, balked at American employees having rights—particularly a right to employment [the model which exists to this day]—and the law was never implemented.

Ironically, Australia enacted a law similar to President Truman's Employment Act—and for the same reason—and for the next 30 years [and until the ill-winds of neo-liberalism in the mid-1970's] Australia's employment model was based on the premise that "anybody wanting to work should be able to find a job"—with 2% or less unemployment common. Australians still refer to this as their "Golden Age".

As a result of the demand by civil rights leaders for legislation, however, in 1978 President Carter signed into law—what is commonly known as the Humphrey-Hawkins Full Employment Act [15 USC § 3101].

The law provides the "legal authorization" for the creation of a "reservoir of public employees" anytime our unemployment in America exceeds "3%". That is, and to this day—at no time should our unemployment rate in America exceed 3%.

The money in politics, however, has prevented this law from being implemented!

Notwithstanding, a lone Congressman, Conyers [and a growing number of co-sponsors] has diligently worked to implement Humphrey-Hawkins [currently, deficit-neutral HR 1000, in Committee].

And, singularly, unemployment is the most pernicious problem facing America, today....

Ref: FULL EMPLOYMENT IS A PRO-MARKET CONCEPT, Amazon

Jim Green, Democrat opponent to Lamar Smith, 2000

Thank You!
Thank you for contacting the White House.

CHAPTER EIGHTEEN

President Obama:

It is impossible to reform our broken criminal justice system—absent our creating a viable job creation program in America.

And while it is generally believed that we do have a job creation program, in fact, we do not!

We have the BELIEF that "the market can provide anybody wanting a job, with a job"—but the data shows that only ONCE since WW II has this belief resulted in an unemployment rate below 3%--in 1953—leaving millions jobless in its wake-- and has resulted in:

60% minority unemployment in our inner-cities, with drug economies, and an epidemic of homicides [i.e., not fixing unemployment has turned our inner-cities into war zones, and created a breeding ground for our inexplicable incarceration rate].

Further this "belief" has been a stumbling block in finding a solution for our pervasive unemployment--In short, we have not been looking for a solution—because our policy makers believe we have one—and apparently few have looked at the data….

Also, ignored in the discussion is that unemployment is a "social" problem, with adverse, and oft severe social consequences—both for the individual, as well as the larger society [i.e., it is the responsibility of the larger society to solve]—

With tentacles integral to all of the social problems facing Americans, today—for instance, ending unemployment is integral to Criminal Justice Reform, and the repair of our crumbling infrastructure….

Further, in 1975 we spent $5 educating our youth, for every $1 we spent on prisons…..by the mid-1990's [with the American people having been terrorized by the Willie Horton ad—and on an hysterical prison building spree] our competing tax dollars tipped in favor of prisons—and at present we spend more on prisons, than on educating our youth.

The irony in all of this is that we have the "legal authorization", on the books to reduce our unemployment rate to 3%, tomorrow [15 USC § 3101—and deficit-neutral HR 1000, currently in Committee]—and also ignored in this context, is that President Obama had a weapon in addressing our economic meltdown in 2008, not available to FDR—and that is the $800 billion in Social Security Insurance claims percolating up through our economy—and in the absence of which--We would be buried in another Great Depression!

Turning the page—and given "automation", alone, is critical going forward in the 21st Century—and is a "win-win"—the American people win, and the market wins….

Ref: FULL EMPLOYMENT IS A PRO-MARKET CONCEPT, Amazon

Jim Green, Democrat opponent to Lamar Smith, 2000

CHAPTER NINETEEN

President Obama/Council of Economic Advisers:

Our network of market-driven economies [the OECD, including the U.S]—currently have a pernicious job creation modality—with resulting high and pervasive unemployment since the mid-1970's—and on a collision course with the future—i.e., given "automation", alone, fewer and fewer jobs are being created with each passing year, as we advance into the 21st Century….

This job creation modality is based on the erroneous propaganda/belief that "the market can provide anybody wanting a job, with a job"—and yet, only ONCE since WW II has this modality resulted in an unemployment rate below 3%--in 1953—leaving millions jobless in its wake, and has resulted in our inner-cities turning into war zones--with 60% minority unemployment, drug economies, and an epidemic of homicides.

The irony in this disaster, however, is that the U.S. correctly anticipated this result in 1978—and provided the American people with a solution, i.e., the "legal authorization" [15 USC § 3101] to limit our unemployment henceforth to "3%", and as we advance into the 21st Century—

With a ton of cash poured into our political system, and a mind-set with both feet planted on the plantation—---

special interests sabotaged this law to prevent its implementation—to the detriment of Americans, and America [ISIS is the least of our worries in America, when we have the Republican party]!

Unemployment is a "social" problem, with adverse social consequences....it is solely the province of the larger society to solve—and leaving the solution to anything as erratic as the market—as we do now—is patently absurd!

The bottom line is that unemployment is a NO ONE WINS....the jobless lose, civility loses, and the market loses, to wit:

THE LAW OF DIMINISHED INCOME TO THE MARKET FROM UNEMPLOYMENT [hereafter D/UE LAW]

3% is the zero-sum threshold above which unemployment triggers inflation by diminishing labor training and skills, under-utilizing capital resources, reducing the rate of productivity advance, increasing unit labor costs, reducing the general supply of goods and services--and the loss in income to the Market is compounded exponentially with each percentage point of increase in unemployment, above 3%.

Ref: HR 1000 [in Committee], and FULL EMPLOYMENT IS A PRO-MARKET SOLUTION, Amazon

Jim Green, Democrat opponent to Lamar Smith, 2000

Thank You!
Thank you for contacting the White House

CHPATER TWENTY

THE HISTORY OF HOW WE GOT WHERE WE ARE
[WW II to Present]

Following WW II, President Truman signed into law the [FULL] EMPLOYMENT ACT of 1946, to provide employment for our returning troops.

Ironically, half-way around the world, Australia codified into their law an almost identical Bill, and for the same reason—

Difference is—Australia actually put their law into effect, and over the next 30 years it was intrinsic to employment policy in Australia that "anybody wanting to work should be able to find a job"—and save for a brief recession in 1961/62 their unemployment was 2%, or less. This period is still referred to as their "Golden Age", in Australia.

Unforeseen by either country, however, in the mid-1970's the world economy underwent a major paradigm shift as a result of the colliding forces of automation, globalization, technology, etc., reaching a critical mass—in brief, an adjustment towards modernity—From a perverse perspective, we became victims of our success....

The instability caused by this transition, however, resulted in a malaise, and ushered in the ill-winds of greed-driven neo-liberalism with its indifference to unemployment, and the likes of Thatcher and Reagan—and the menace of this greed-driven agenda was exploded by Bush II, resulting in obscene disparities in wealth that persists, and is the cause of much friction between right and left, to this day.

It also ushered in high and pervasive unemployment throughout our market-driven economies, the OECD—with 6% unemployment in Australia now the norm, and double-digit unemployment common throughout the Eurozone, to this day.

As a result of the "malaise", however, the U.S. took an aggressive, pro-active role in addressing the, above, economic shift—and in 1978 President Carter signed into law one of the most important laws in the 20th Century--an expansion of President Truman's full employment, i.e., Pro-Market 15 USC § 3101--which provides a "*legal authorization*" to create a "reservoir of public employees" [*indispensable to the effective functioning of a 21st Century market economy*]--at any time our unemployment in America exceeds "3%"—

But in spite of 3% unemployment being the threshold point above which unemployment starts substantially undermining the Market—this *legal authorization* has never been implemented--

And in spite of deficit-neutral HR 1000, or The Neighbor-To-Neighbor Job Creation Act—A federally mandated Social Insurance, owned by our employed, to provide a fund to hire/train our unemployed—[more on the critical need to apply this job creation methodology in a 21st Century market economy, ahead]….

Ref: **FULL EMPLOYMENT IS A PRO-MARKET CONCEPT, Amazon/Kindle**

Jim Green, Democrat opponent to Lamar Smith, Congress, 2000

CHAPTER TWENTY-ONE

THE HISTORY OF HOW WE GOT WHERE WE ARE

[Mid-1970's to Present]

In the mid-1970's, the colliding forces of automation, technology, globalization, etc., reached a critical mass—resulting in a Market no longer capable of producing the jobs necessary to its viability, and causing ubiquitous unemployment in all of the OECD countries—and leaving their leaders conflicted, ever since, regarding the displaced employee. Eurozone unemployment is still in double digits, and Greece and Spain both in excess of 20%, plus. High unemployment was also a major factor in Arab Spring.

In the U.S., we took a pro-active role in addressing this economic shift—and in 1978 President Carter signed into law 15 USC § 3101--which "authorizes" the creation of a "reservoir of public employment" at any time our unemployment in America exceeds "3%".

In 1979, however, and in a panic over Humphrey-Hawkins—our ultra-conservative foundations, and desperate to promote the Supply-Side fraud, embraced a flawed paper by an obscure MIT student, David L. Birch "The Job Generation Process"; and [with lots of cash] gave his paper biblical importance, and every president since has cited his finding as gospel.

Birch's paper concluded that "small businesses" were the greatest generator of new jobs—problem is, for the purposes of policy-making—it is BS. In a study at Harvard University in 2010, "The Myth of Small Business Job Creation" The research shows "no systematic relationship between firm size and growth." And that small businesses can actually detract from job growth.

In spite of this, however, Washington struggles, still, to make this antiquated notion, work--that it is only the market that can create jobs—and the result has been a disaster, politically as well as otherwise!

It would be impossible to still have 7.8% unemployment—if we were on the right path—and among other problems with this concept--if the market fails, the unemployed are out of luck.

Further, unemployment is a "social" problem we are seeking to address with a highly unstable, incompatible entity: The Market

What apparently isn't clear going forward is that an expanding and contracting public workforce is an *indispensable* component to the *effective* functioning of a modern market economy—

The market thrives when we have a robust, employed, consuming workforce—and overlooked is that HR 1000 [currently in Committee], and the proposed "Neighbor-To-Neighbor Job Creation Act" www.Inclusivism.org [both authorized under Humphrey-Hawkins], are deficit-neutral--Pro-Market "win-win" solutions:

The American people win, and capitalism wins—

Jim Green, Democrat candidate for Congress, 2000

CHAPTER TWENTY-TWO

Friends: In the event you have gotten this far—according to the Federal Election Commission, I am a candidate for president in the 2016 election—and rest assured I am not delusional, or like Trump…on an ego trip…..I filed solely to deliver a message—you are reading it—and to urge passage of the above legislation….

To Whom It May Concern—in Washingon:

OUR CHOICES ARE: Adapt and change in a world that is changing, whether we like it or not, OR be forced to create a Police State to hold our anachronistic policies, practices and laws in place—

And in America, today, we have chosen the latter…..and as only one pernicious example, of thousands—Ferguson is the result….

In a comedic, but religious context we hear of persons asking God for a sign—anything—which will warn us that we are on the wrong path, and need to change direction…..and our Police State choice, above, is *our sign*…..few are listening….

To illustrate a critical area in which we need to adapt and change in a 21st Century economy: We have far more work that needs to be done in America, than we have persons to fill these jobs—And 86% of Americans believe that "Anybody wanting to work should be able to find a job"---So, why on earth *in a democracy*, do we have 9 million jobless Americans—[per the 11/14 DOL Jobs report]?

The answer is because our *method* of job creation in America is based on a Fairy Tale! Specifically, our current *one and only* job creation methodology in America, is based on the myth/sacred cow:

"The market can provide anybody wanting a job, with a job"—

Problem is—it is pure BS—and only *once* since WW II has this methodology resulted in an unemployment rate below 3%--in 1953 [i.e., which translates into 5 million left jobless]--because the market *cannot* create enough jobs—in short, the jobs for this 5 million jobless--*don't exist*!

The right-wing propaganda mills trick our fools into believing that the market has created this 5 million jobs, but because those on welfare are "lazy and don't want to work" this 5 million jobs go unfilled—but that is *pure balderdash!*

The vast majority of persons on welfare, are there *because* the *market* cannot create enough jobs, i.e., the market lacks the viability to create these jobs—the jobs simply *do not exist*!

And as further proof, according to the CBO, on our current path it will be 2017 before America returns to even an anemic 5.5% unemployment rate [following the Great Recession] and if the market fails in the interim—the jobless are out of luck!

Further, this travesty is compounded because the Republicans cling to devious and discredited Supply Side Economics [to this day] as a solution, to wit:

Siphon America's wealth away from the consuming middle—give this windfall of cash to the Koch Bros [a metaphor for the 1%, hereafter "KB"]—they will build factories all across our fair land—everyone will have a job in the corporation—and we will all live happily ever after—Yes, folks it is a fairy tale!

And what we learned from this dark cloud over America is what Bush I called it long ago—before America was subjected to this devious scam—i.e., Supply-Side is "VooDoo Economics"!

So why have we allowed ourselves to be deceived by this Republican scam—[handcrafted by a plutocracy/oligarchy that still has one foot on the plantation]? But I don't want to giveaway the surprise ending—and some of my response isn't printable....! Further, and to say it up front....I am a capitalist—I support 100%: Build a better widget, sell it for a million bucks, and retire in South Florida....it is the Republican agenda, today, that is anti-market...more on this throughout.....

When President Carter handed the reigns over to Reagan in 1981—he left America with a very modest $60 billion deficit—as a direct result of Supply-Side, however, when Republicans held the White House [Clinton actually cut the deficit]—this $60 billion ballooned to a staggering $10 trillion by 2008—and it has cost Americans an additional $7+trillion to clean up this Republican mess—

Ask any economist: Our only way out of a meltdown *is to buy our way out!* [it was the lesson learned from the Great Depression].

And anyone who thinks McCain, had he been elected, would not have addressed this with a Stimulus, the same as President Obama in 2009—is stuffed between the ears with rice pudding......

Further, we learned that we cannot siphon America's wealth away from the consuming middle, and give it to the "KB"—without sending our economy into meltdown—as occurred in 1987 and 2008—in short, the Supply-Side scam has a shelf-life of about 7 years before the economy collapses—and as noted, costing the taxpayers trillions to put a floor under a disappearing economy!

And another fallout/direct result from this dark chapter is the disparity in wealth it has created in America—AKA the "wealth gap"--and currently the "richest 1 percent in the United States now own more wealth than the bottom 90 percent"—the second highest in our history, the first was just before the Great Depression.

A couple of other factors that played into the above scenario—when every waking moment in capitalism is spent pondering how to eliminate as many of us humans, as possible, from the workplace—to increase "profits"—why, on Earth, would we look to the market to solve our unemployment crisis in America?

As well, few things on earth are more unstable than the market….we can count on one hand the number of corporations in America that were around in 1900….with tens of thousands long since disappeared; and given "automation", alone, the market will produce fewer and fewer jobs the further we advance into the 21st Century.

Further, unemployment is a "social" problem—we, as the larger society have the responsibility to solve—i.e., it is unrealistic to expect the market to solve this problem—the market is in the "for profit" business, not the social work business—and the former would not long be in business--if they were…for example, we should never condemn the CEO for closing a plant when they are losing money—but we should be outraged by a government that doesn't have a clue re the displaced employees…..

Also, unemployment is a _no one wins_ …..the jobless lose, and market loses, to wit:

3% is the zero-sum threshold above which unemployment triggers inflation by diminishing labor training and skills, under-utilizing capital resources, reducing the rate of productivity advance, increasing unit labor costs, and reducing the general supply of goods and services--and the loss in income to the Market is compounded exponentially with each percentage point of increase in unemployment, above 3%.

Short Definition:

3% is the zero-sum threshold above which unemployment starts substantially undermining the Market--and the loss in income to the Market is compounded exponentially with each percentage point of increase in unemployment, above 3%.

In sum, our job creation should be based on: Fix unemployment, and this will fix the market [HR 1000], rather than [our current mind-set] Fix the market, and this in turn fix unemployment [HR 2847] – with a result that has been a disaster—as we inch along in our job recovery, see data above, and when we didn't *Fix Unemployment* a retaliatory electorate ushered in a House filled with lunatics in the 2010 election, and then doubled down in 2014!

Look around—all signs in our economy are up—and yet over two-thirds of our rank and file believe "we are moving in the wrong direction"—their perception is that our economy is in the tank—that we are in an economic malaise—a condition that would disappear overnight if we did, in fact, *Fix Unemployment*!

Best guess is that Congress passed, and President Obama signed into law HR 2847 [the HIRE Act], in 2009—which is based on fix the market, and this will fix unemployment [180 degrees off course]—but they did this because of the pervasive [but false] *belief* that "The market can provide anybody wanting a job, with a job"—it is *pure BS......it doesn't work*! Had we insisted on putting a lawnmower engine in the rocket to get us to the Moon....we would never have gotten there...[same difference]....and all of the empirical evidence is proof HR 2847 didn't create anywhere near the jobs needed...

Jim Green, Democrat opponent to Lamar Smith, Congress, 2000

CHAPTER TWENTY-THREE

HOPPER-READY: THE NEIGHBOR-TO-NEIGHBOR JOB CREATION ACT

[1] PROPOSED LEGISLATION:

THE NEIGHBOR-TO-NEIGHBOR JOB CREATION ACT

A Pro-Market, deficit-neutral, federally mandated, Social Insurance, owned by our employed, to provide a fund to hire/train our unemployed.

SECTION 1. SHORT TITLE.

> This Act shall be cited as The Neighbor-To-Neighbor Job Creation Act [To establish employment/training opportunities for the unemployed in compliance with the "Legal Authorization" in Public Law 15 USC § 3101, for the creation of a "reservoir of public employees", anytime our unemployment rate exceeds "3%", with an emphasis on training for market needs, including a training stipend, where there is a shortage of trained workers--hereafter NTN].

SEC. 2. DEFINITIONS.

In this Act the following definitions apply:

(1) SECRETARY- The term `Secretary' means the Secretary of Labor.

(2) STATE- The term `State' has the meaning given such term in section 102(2) of the Housing and Community Development Act (42 U.S.C. 5302(2)).

(3) TRUST FUND- The term `Trust Fund' refers to the Department of Labor Full Employment Trust Fund.

(4) UNIT OF GENERAL LOCAL GOVERNMENT- The term `unit of general local government' has the meaning given such term in section 102(1) of the Housing and Community Development Act (42 U.S.C. 5302(1)).

(5) URBAN COUNTY- The term `urban county' has the meaning given such term in section 102(6) of the Housing and Community Development Act (42 U.S.C. 5302(6)).

(6) WEB SITE- The Secretary shall establish an Internet Web site to serve as an information clearinghouse for job training and employment opportunities funded by the Trust Fund.

SEC. 3. EMPLOYMENT OPPORTUNITY GRANTS TO STATES, LOCAL GOVERNMENT.

(a) Use of Funds-A recipient of a grant under this section shall use the grant primarily for infrastructure repair, including, but not limited to:

(A) The painting and repair of schools, community centers, and libraries.
(B) The restoration and revitalization of abandoned and vacant properties to alleviate blight in distressed and foreclosure-affected areas of a unit of general local government.
(C) The augmentation of staffing in Head Start, child care, and other early childhood education programs to promote school readiness and early literacy.
(D) The renovation and enhancement of maintenance of parks, playgrounds, and other public spaces.

Respectfully Submitted,

Jim Green, Democrat candidate for Congress, Dist 21, TX, 2000

CHAPTER TWENTY-FOUR

WHAT WE NEED TO DO GOING FORWARD IN THE 21ST CENTURY:

Inexplicably "public employment" is seen the same as WPA—where millions are employed directly by the federal government—when that model is not only outmoded—it is insufficient to address our problems in the 21st century.

What we need today is an expanding and contracting public workforce—that expands during downturns in the market, and contracts as employees return to the private sector [Google: The Buffer Stock Employment Model]—triggered anytime our unemployment exceeds "3%" [as "authorized" under Humphrey-Hawkins]-- and least understood: This is an INDISPENSABLE component in the effective functioning of our 21st Century Market.

The market thrives when we have a robust, employed, consuming workforce—our manufacturers are sitting on $2 trillion in cash because they do not have consumers for their products—i.e., absent consumers, they lay off employees—[and the Republican solution, Reaganomics, has acted as an accelerate to this downward spiral—and which Romney promises to return us to if he is elected]!

In short, the above model is a "win-win" solution—the American people win, and capitalism wins!

To achieve this, what is being urged is "The Neighbor-To-Neighbor Job Creation Act": A federally mandated, mutual insurance—owned by our employed [from janitor to CEO] to create a fund to hire/train our unemployed.

To be viable, however, our job creation solution _MUST_ contain:

1] Be based on the premise that we have far more work that needs to be done in America, than we have persons to fill these jobs.

2] It MUST have renewable funding.

3] It will not add a dime to our deficit.

To expand briefly, it is currently believed, erroneously, that we need "make work" jobs so that everyone who wants to work will have a job—but this is absurd—and an insult to "Yankee Ingenuity".

We do not have an unemployment crisis from a shortage of jobs, or money—but rather from a shortage of imagination.

Regarding "renewable funding" ALL of our job creation solutions, to date, have been based on the mind-set: "jump start" the market, and the market will in turn create all the jobs we need—and even setting aside that this is untrue, our current job creation is moving at a snail's pace—long past the unemployment benefits drying up—with the CBO projecting that even with the JOBS Act, signed into law on April 6, 2012--it will be 2017 before we return to a barely acceptable 5.5% unemployment rate!

Further, by its nature when we "jump start" --the employment ends when the funding runs out as we learned from the Stimulus—whereas any real fix to our unemployment crisis *demands* renewable funding….

And whether the electorate will accept an unemployment rate hovering around 8% on election day—is the $64,000 question….

Regarding not adding a dime to our deficit—under The Neighbor-To-Neighbor Job Creation Act [NTN], the *funding* to reduce our unemployment to 3% comes from an insurance owned by our employed, rather than added to our deficit—

If one is employed in America, participation in this insurance plan is mandatory—similar in concept to our auto insurance or Social Security Insurance [and without question the most successful social program in American history].

Jobs beget jobs--And with a modest policy cost of 4% of salary we can create more "private-sector" jobs in 6 months, that HR 2847, and the JOBS Act, in 6 years—and unlike these laws—NTN will not add a dime to our deficit!

Finally, this is in total concert with the will of the American people, i.e., that "anybody willing to work should be able to find a job"—and the American people have told our politicians time and again of their willingness to chip in to help their neighbor get a job [and as an *insurance*, as above, it also protects their continued employment]—it is just that Washington is deaf as an adder!

CHAPTER TWENTY-FIVE

President Obama/Council of Economic Advisers:

Public-Sector jobs strengthen our free-enterprise market economy—i.e., they are a critical component to the viability of our 21st Century economy--rather than weakening the market--as propagandist, with one foot on the plantation, fraudulently deceive the public into believing for the purposes of exploiting American employees…..

Indeed, since WW II, the Koch brothers [both literally, and a metaphor, here, for the 1%] have spent tens of millions buying governors and legislators, to cement "at will" employment in every state [and currently only Montana limits to probationary employees]; and to destroy "collective bargaining", i.e., unions in America—

In sum, they have spent tens of millions of dollars to destroy "employee rights" in America!

To understand the importance of "collective bargaining" for employees, it is informative to take a page from history:

When Hitler became the dictator in Germany, one of his first laws was to make it illegal for more than three persons to gather on the street—and German citizens were subject to immediate arrest if they did.

The same principal is being used by preventing employees putting their heads together, as it were, to bargain for employee rights—and recently one group of employees placed "job security" over a salary increase—with the irony being that the specific objective of "at will" employment—is to destroy "job security"!

In short, the deceptive propaganda to frighten Americans regarding "public-sector" jobs, has but a single parent: To exploit American labor—by some, to assuage deep-seated feelings of inferiority [they can only feel tall, by making others small, in their eyes]-— but most often for just pure GREED!

Where our policies makers go wrong by pandering to some in the oligarchy—and/or buying into this fraudulent propaganda:

Unemployment is a NO ONE WINS—the jobless lose, civility loses, and the market loses, to wit:

THE LAW OF DIMINISHED INCOME TO THE MARKET FROM UNEMPLOYMENT [hereafter D/UE LAW]

Short Definition:

> 3% is the zero-sum threshold above which unemployment starts substantially undermining the Market--and the loss in income to the Market is compounded exponentially with each

percentage point of increase in unemployment, above 3%.

Ref: IT IS IMPOSSIBLE TO BE A CHRISTIAN, AND VOTE REPUBLICAN, Amazon

Jim Green, Democrat opponent to Lamar Smith, 2000

CHAPTER TWENTY-SIX

FAIL-SAFE ELECTRONIC VOTING

TO THE READER: Given you have gotten this far, and agree with the proposed changes—and particularly given the pernicious Citizens United—our democracy, and the above, or any, progress, will be in peril absent a "fail-safe" electronic voting system. The following is my proposed solution, and like every solution proposed, here, feed-back--your proposed improvement, etc. is welcomed:

THE FAIL-SAFE ELECTRONIC VOTING ACT

1) EVERY electronic voting machine (hereafter EVM), must be inexpensive, identical throughout the U.S. in a 1/150 ratio, and *must count and produce a hard-copy of the recorded votes.* In addition, an extra copy of their recorded votes would be produced (not necessarily a hard-copy), marked "Voter's Copy", and containing "NOTICE: Do Not Destroy Until Every Election On Your Ballot Is Certified". [If Wal-Mart handed us a piece of paper with the words "trust us" as a receipt for our purchases—we would be outraged—and yet, this is our current electronic voting nightmare—but in this case it is our democracy at risk]!

2) *After confirming that their votes are recorded correctly*, the voter would then insert the hard-copy ballot into a software-free (count only) optical scanner (hereafter OS), for a second count. The hard-copy

ballot would be retained by election officials in the event a candidate asks for a recount (*<u>not possible under the current system, and which undermines the legality of each such election</u>*). The EVM and the OS must be manufactured by different companies (which is universally true today).

3) Election officials assigned to oversee the EVM, would be prevented by law from overseeing the OS, and vice-versa, and stiff criminal penalties would be imposed for violations.

4) Further, every EVM would be programmed with raw data re the total registration rolls, by party, and norms for their voting history, etc.,----as an "alert" to a possible irregularity, such as an "under-vote"—or "vote-flipping" etc., and <u>standards</u> established to suspend certification where there is an "improbable result", at least temporarily, of a particular election until the discrepancy is cleared up. (This is what computers do best, and it would be very easy to create such a program).

5) At the end of the election day, tallies would be taken from the EVM and the OS, for each candidate. *If the tallies didn't balance for any given election, or if there is an "alert", that election cannot be certified until the "error" is corrected.* If the candidates agree (the victory is certain), minor discrepancies in the count could be disregarded. While probably rare, the Voter, or a random sample of Voters, would be required by law to return their Copy of the recorded votes to the election

office to clear up any "error", or where an "alert" signals the need for same.

6) Further, every state provides for a recount when the total vote falls below a certain percent of difference between the candidates, impossible to conduct with the current EVM. And thus Congress must mandate the following regarding presidential candidates: A RUN-OFF election is mandated and triggered in those states where the percent of total vote is less than .5% of difference between the two candidates; said election to be held on the second Saturday following the election, on PAPER BALLOTS ONLY, and contain ONLY the names of the relevant candidates, for instance: "Barack Obama, Democrat" and "John McCain, Republican"—with oversight in counting by a representative(s) of each party—said procedure providing more than adequate time to meet the Electoral College mandate [Ideally, all of this could be eliminated if we did away with the Electoral College, but until then….]. NOTE: Had this been the law in 2000, Al Gore would be our president, and America would have been spared the economic, etc., disaster that followed!

7) Finally, absent the above safeguards, and until these safeguards are in place--Congress must mandate that PAPER BALLOTS, ONLY, can be used in our presidential elections. This is not a "partisan" issue, it is a "pro-democracy" issue. Most importantly, this will return the responsibility for our elections, and our vote counting, back into the hands of the individual voter, where it belongs, and out of the hands of "corporate control"---*it is* *after all "our democracy", itself, that is at*

risk if we don't take these steps---and in that regard, is there any time or cost differential that is too great?

Jim Green

CHAPTER TWENTY-SEVEN

I didn't write the following. It is a cut and paste from FACEBOOK, or some blog [would like to give credit if knew the author]--but it is so on target regarding how "fear" is driving Conservative policy in America today—i.e., is undermining America and our progress—and relegating America to a Third World country status, rather than a world leader—FDR had it on the nose in "All we have to fear, is fear itself"...at his inaugural in 1933....

"Conservatives are such cowards: they are afraid of gay people getting married or serving in the military; they are afraid of bringing terrorists to super max prisons in the US from which no one has ever escaped; they are afraid of the boy scouts letting gay kids in; they are afraid of everyone voting and are constantly suppressing the vote under some bogus voter fraud theory; they are afraid of letting students vote at their universities; they are afraid of women having the right to choose; they even are afraid of women getting contraception [the real issue actually is a women's agency and control over their bodies]; they are afraid of immigration reform leading to citizenship because they are afraid of-- name whatever reason; they are afraid of mandating gun purchasers to undergo background checks for crazy people and terrorists; they are afraid of people smoking pot; they are afraid of climate change being real and contradicting their beloved Bible; they are afraid of legitimate campaign reform; they are afraid of Muslims; they are afraid of blacks; they are afraid of atheists; they are afraid of hippies; they are afraid of socialists; they are probably still afraid of monsters under their beds; they are just rank cowards and keep making things up to be afraid of."

CHAPTER TWENTY-EIGHT

[I couldn't resist including this...and yes I am the author…..]

A MESSAGE FROM GOD

MANY CENTURIES AGO, a man of the cloth, we don't know his name, and in a flash of insight (perhaps induced by peyote) told his flock that "sex is a sin". And lo and behold he learned that by taking a very natural and healthy part of our life and turning it into something that was "dirty and nasty", that he could imprison his flock, and fill his coffers, and hallelujah it was a great day for the Lord!

Quickly, his miracle spread to other churches in his village, and then to the next village, and then the next county, and then state, and soon it spread to all the churches in the ancient world, and all of their flocks cowed in fear and shame and became imprisoned, and their coffers over-floweth. Hallelujah, it was a great day for the Lord!

And to keep the myth alive they started inventing stories, half-baked stories, that made no sense to anyone who is rational, such as "Mary was a virgin"—well, she just had to be a virgin because she would never partake in anything that was dirty and nasty, like sex (if you're doing it right), and this was necessary to make "sex is a sin" make sense...so they invented a Mary that was "sinless"--you get the picture. And their coffers over-floweth. Hallelujah, it was a great day for the Lord!

No one seemed to be bothered that when we play tricks on the human mind by taking something that is very natural and healthy, such as sex, and make it dirty and nasty that all kinds of bad things happen to the human mind:

Such as most pedophiles, and most serial killers, and voting Republican, and unwarranted suicides, and most mental illness, and unwanted pregnancies. (Teens not wanting to have sex is the perversion, not the other way around, and by replacing sex education and condoms, with unrealistic "abstinence", and by using blather about "low self-esteem" to shame them into not "sinning"—We have a teen pregnancy in the U.S. twice that of England and Canada!).

But none of this mattered, because their coffers over-floweth, and Hallelujah, it is a great day for the Lord!

There is a cure--------Tell our right-wing hypocrites, who Judge, rather than "Judge not"…. to shove it….

GOD

ABOUT THE AUTHOR: I was employed in our Criminal Justice System for a cumulative 20 years as a probation officer, with 5 of those years as a chief probation officer. I authored the concept of "Shock Incarceration" which became law in Kansas in 1970, and then was adopted in numerous jurisdictions in the U.S. and also spread to Europe—it is currently identified in the U.S. as "Boot Camp" [as the means to "shock" the young offender—and a total distortion of my original intent—like many ideas, once released, they take on a life of their own]. I also instigated establishment of the first Court Psychiatric Clinic in the U.S., in conjunction with psychiatrists from the Menninger Foundation, as a chief probation officer. Finally, I was the Democrat candidate for Congress, District 21, TX, 2000. I would most define myself as a Social Ecologist-- [albeit my degree is in Psychology]. My web page is www.Inclusivism.org –which has been on the internet since 1996.
http://www.amazon.com/James-L.-Jim-Green/e/B001KHZIMM/ref=ntt_dp_epwbk_0

A BRIEF ADDENDUM: When the U.S. Supreme Court denied certiorari—where the violation of my constitutional rights were obvious, and criminal negligence on the part of the government defendants in the death of our son, equally obvious—[detailed in THE HARVARD BOYS CLUB, Amazon/Kindle]--I filed a Petition for Rehearing [which is automatic]—and included the following. The Clerk of the U.S. Supreme Court called me at my work in California, and asked that I withdraw the "cartoon" [a reprint from The NEW YORKER] from my Petition. I refused on the basis of the First Amendment, and it remains in the archives at the U.S. Supreme Court [Docket #: 79-1627], to this day. The wording [not that clear] is: "Excellent, excellent. A fine blend of truths, half-truths, and blatant falsehoods".

IN THE

Supreme Court of the United States

October Term, 1979

No. <u>79-1627</u>

JAMES L. GREEN,   Petitioner,

vs.

"Excellent, excellent. A fine blend of truths, half-truths, and blatant falsehoods."

OTHER BOOKS BY THIS AUTHOR ON AMAZON/KINDLE/BN:

- **THE HARVARD BOYS CLUB:** Hitler's Assault On Our Freedoms From His Grave
- **MY LETTERS TO PRESIDENT OBAMA:** Confessions Of A Compulsive Letter Writer
- **OUR GREED AND IGNORANCE:** Poses A Far Greater Threat To America, Than Terrorism
- **LETTERS ON STEROIDS:** Confessions Of A Compulsive Letter-To-The-Editor Writer
- **THE FIRST TIME I HAD SEX:** And, The Religious Intolerance Attack On America
- **WHY PRESIDENT OBAMA LOST THE 2012 ELECTION:** A Wake-Up Call
- **ECONOMIC INCLUSIVISM:** Neo-Capitalism/An Anthology: Inclusive pro-market solutions to our social problems
- **AMERICA IS ONE SICK MF:** Why Greed-Driven America Went Off The Rails….
- **EVERY GIVEN SUNDAY:** A Scientific Formula To Predict NFL Games

And others….http://www.amazon.com/James-L.-Jim-Green/e/B001KHZIMM/ref=ntt_dp_epwbk_0

www.ingramcontent.com/pod-product-compliance
Lightning Source LLC
Chambersburg PA
CBHW020927180526
45163CB00007B/2909